We Can Cook

Written by Sophia Payne

Illustrated by Sayada Ramdial

Collins

This is a good pot for cooking.

Look at all we need for cooking dinner.

3

Chop the garlic.

Put it in the pot.

Now add it all to the pot.

6

Wait for the pot to boil.

The food is cooking.

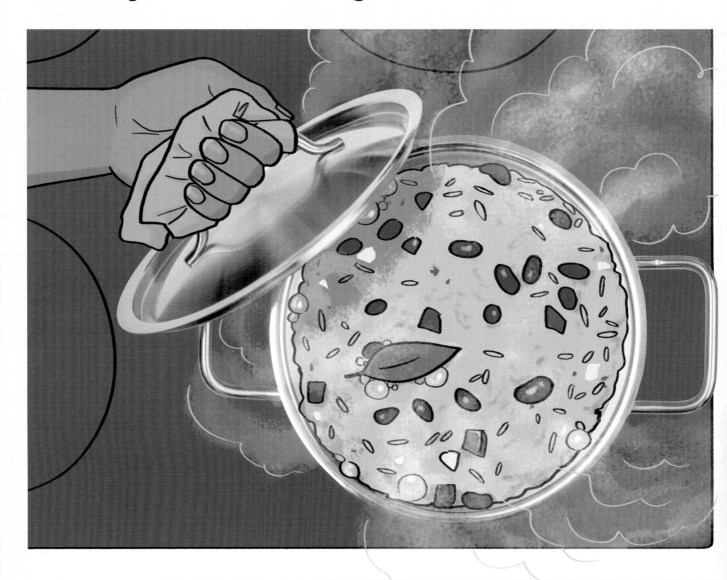

Dinner will be soon!

This is how we cook jerk chicken.
It cooks on coal.

We are all waiting for dinner.

I hear the bell ringing.

Dinner looks good!

Cooking dinner

15

Review: After reading

Use your assessment from hearing the children read to choose any GPCs, words or tricky words that need additional practice.

Read 1: Decoding

- Ask the children to read page 7, then check their understanding of the meaning of **boil**. Ask: What happens when a pot boils? (e.g. *the food inside the pot gets hot enough to bubble*)
- Point to the word **food** on page 8. Ask the children to sound out the letters in the word, then blend. (*f/oo/d* – **food**) Repeat for **cooking** and check they sound out the shorter /**oo**/ sound. (*c/**oo**/k/i/ng* – **cooking**). Point to **soon** on page 9 and ask them to sound out the letters, then blend. Check they use the longer /oo/ sound.

Read 2: Prosody

- Read pages 4 and 5 using different tones and emphasising different words.
- Encourage the children to read the pages in an instructional voice.
- Encourage them to emphasise the imperative verbs to make the instructions clear.

Read 3: Comprehension

- Discuss favourite cooked meals that the children eat or would like to eat. Ask: What different things are in the meal? What might you need to cook them?
- Reread pages 8 and 10. Talk about the ways in which the different foods are cooked. Ask: What do you think is in the pot? (e.g. *vegetables, rice and beans*) How is the chicken cooked? (e.g. *on coal on a barbecue*)
- Turn to pages 14 and 15. Talk about the stages involved in cooking the meal. Use the pictures as prompts for describing each stage in sequence.